Baminals

Baminals
All Creatures Big and Boggin'

Scott Simpson

BLACK & WHITE PUBLISHING

First published 2007
by Black & White Publishing Ltd
99 Giles Street, Edinburgh, EH6 6BZ

ISBN 13: 978 1 84502 185 6
ISBN 10: 1 84502 185 1

A CIP catalogue record for this book is available from The
British Library.

Typeset by AJT
Printed and bound in Poland
www.polskabook.pl

Acknowledgements

First and foremost, I owe a huge debt of gratitude (as well as a few beers) to Joni Hawley and his electronic difference engine for bringing the Baminals to life.

Thanks must also go to Shona, Dean, Emma, Joanne, Kirsty, Leigh, Neil Stevenson and everyone at Black & White Publishing.

For my auld man.

A foreword by Charles Darwin (deceased)

When Mr Simpson first contacted me by means of a clairvoyant and asked if I would be so kind as to write a foreword for his book on Scottish wildlife, I was hesitant to say the least. Surely he understood that his being able to contact me on the 'other side', so to speak, was a fact which lent itself to the notion that God did exist and, therefore, that the theory of evolution to which I had devoted the best years of my life was nothing more than a load of old poo. It wasn't until he explained that this book would cover the subject of Baminals that I fully understood. For, as you are probably only too well aware, Baminals are the only forms of life on earth that God had absolutely nothing to do with. In fact, not even Beelzebub himself is willing to take the credit for them.

I, on the other hand, have had some experience in the field of Baminals, having studied at Edinburgh University back in the 1820s. It was there that I first encountered a strange and wonderful creature called a Jakey. Every morning, on my way to lectures, I would stroll past this Jakey lying in a shop doorway in a pool of its own vomit and urine and, as I would pass by, the Jakey would look up at me and growl something that sounded like 'Yawrightpal', which I later learned was a form of greeting. I was fascinated by this creature and took it upon myself to study it in more detail. A few weeks later I was able to translate some of its grunts and whistles into English. For example, the correct response to 'Yawrightpal' is 'Aye nobad – howzyersel?' After that, however, things began to get a tad repetitive. I was also intrigued by the Jakey's ability to remain in a state of constant inebriation despite having no visible means of income. This was later explained by the way the good people of Edinburgh would offer the Jakey small sums of money in return for being left alone.

Turning my attention to other species of Baminals that inhabit Scotland, I discovered, amongst others: a small furry beast that steals ladies' undergarments from washing lines called a Plampher; a Snottery Beak, which is a repulsive snail-like creature that secretes a sticky green substance from its nose; and a small blue and white Baminal known as a Nasher who, upon hearing my English accent, blamed me for its own pitiful existence and threatened to kick my head in.

I'm ashamed to say that, while observing the Baminals of Scotland, I had neglected my own studies and I was unceremoniously booted out of Edinburgh University a few years later. I returned home to England and soon forgot all about the northern beasts. This book, however, goes a long way to finishing what I started almost 200 years ago and I hope you find it as enjoyable and informative as I might if I were still alive.

Best wishes,
Charles Darwin
Heaven

The Snottery Beak

Snottery Beaks are wretchedly unpopular creatures who have been cursed with overactive nasal glands that secrete a sticky green fluid. Consequently, they are doomed to wander the earth, forever in search of a handkerchief or long-sleeved shirt.

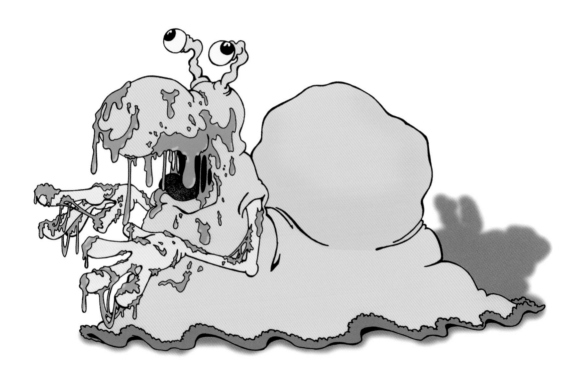

The Snottery Beak

The Crabbit

Commonly found in all parts of Scotland, the Crabbit is probably the only member of the baminal kingdom that is born in a bad mood and remains in a state of ill-tempered pessimism for the remainder of its miserable life. Crabbits have the ability to find fault in almost everything they encounter but, if there is one thing that the crabbit cannot bear above all else, it is the sound of children's laughter. So much so that they will often hide behind their curtains for days on end in the hope that a happy child might wander by. Once its prey is within earshot, the crabbit will throw back the curtains, lean out the window and bellow, 'WILL YOU KEEP THE BLOODY NOISE DOON? I CANNAE HEAR MAH TELLY FUR YOU WEE BUGGERS!'

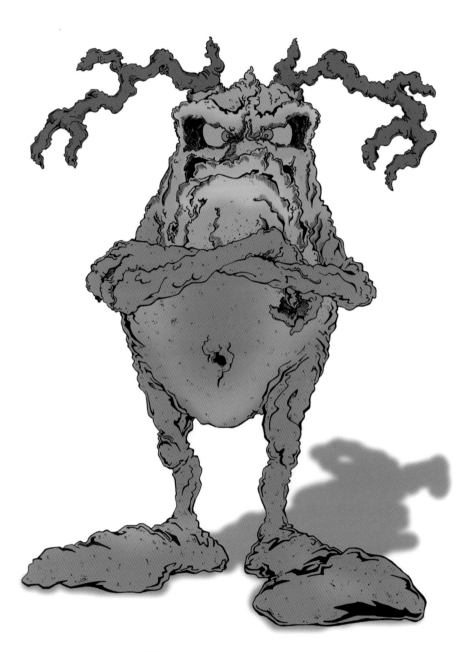

The Crabbit

The Jakey

Jakeys are just as much a part of Scotland's national identity as haggis, shortbread and chronic heart disease. For as far back as can be remembered, these slightly wobbly creatures have staggered across the country, knocking back their cans of super strength lager, urinating in full view of men, women and children and roaring incoherent abuse at invisible people. Despite their outwardly fearsome appearance, Jakeys are essentially friendly creatures who seem genuinely concerned for the well-being of others, as evidenced by the fact that they will often follow you for miles asking if you are all right and attempting to shake you warmly by the hand.

The Jakey

The Clype

Seemingly unsolvable mysteries, such as 'Who broke that window?', 'Who spilled blackcurrant juice on the living room carpet?' and 'Who put the gerbil in the microwave?', can normally be solved with the assistance of a Clype. Clypes keep an ever-watchful eye on children that might be getting up to mischief and report back to mothers, teachers and the police. Although Clypes are born with a full set of teeth, they normally have them kicked out by the time they reach puberty in revenge for their despicable actions.

The Clype

The Beamer

The Beamer is something of a rarity in Scotland in as much as it is one of the few Baminals that prefers not to make a complete arse of itself whenever possible. Beamers are not particularly bright and, when they inevitably make a fool of themselves, their enlarged faces become flushed and give off enough heat to strip the paint off doors. Scientists at Glasgow University are looking at ways to harness the energy given off by these creatures and believe that a single Beamer, with a bit of toilet paper stuck to its foot, might generate enough energy to run twenty-five thousand deep-fat fryers for a week.

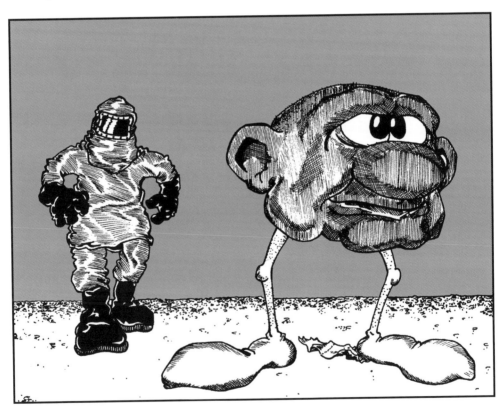

The Beamer

The Nasher

The Nasher, or Nationalist to give him his full name, believes himself to be a true Scottish patriot whereas, in actual fact, he is just another small-minded racist who makes the late Bernard Manning look like a bleeding-heart liberal – so much so that his patriotism is measured not by how much he loves Scotland but by how much he hates the English. The average Nasher's account of Scottish history is somewhat skewed and many believe that William Wallace defeated the armies of King Henry VIII at the Battle of Culloden in 1066 which, incidentally, was the year after he married Mary Queen of Scots and invented the telephone.

The Nasher

The Chore

If you have your eye on the latest state-of-the-art DVD player but don't want to pay the going rate, you might want to employ the services of a Chore. Chores are resourceful little creatures who can liberate anything from a packet of batteries to a 52-inch plasma-screen television from the shelves of a high-street retailer and sell it on to you at a fraction of the cost. Sadly, thanks to improvements in electronic stock tagging and thorough background checks on security personnel, Chores are finding it increasingly hard to make a living and many are now kept in captivity.

The Chore

The Numpty

Not everyone who arrives at Glasgow airport with third degree burns on 95% of their body is neccessarily looking for a square go with a baggage handler. Every year thousands of Scottish Numpties return from their holidays abroad looking as though they have been bungee jumping off the lip of a volcano.

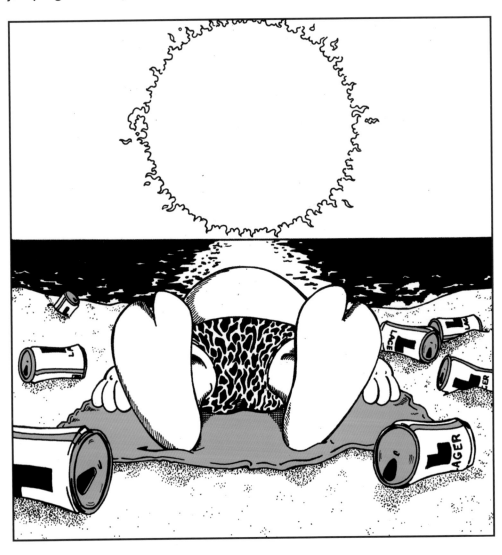

The Numpty

The Bam

If there's one sight that is guaranteed to stir the blood of any true Scotsman, then it has to be that of a fully grown Bam rearing up on its hind legs and roaring at the moon. This monarch of the housing scheme, fuelled by alcohol and testosterone, has become something of an icon, mainly for people with shit for brains, though even Robert Burns himself felt compelled to write a poem in its honour:

> Doon at the chippy, the Bams are feedin'
> and lookin tae kick somebody's heid in.
> Among the blood and among the snotters,
> the Bam rears up on its hind trotters
> and, with a mooth full o' broken glass,
> bellows, 'Come ahead, ya bass!'

While it's wise to maintain a safe distance from the Bam, they can be observed in chip shop queues after 11.30 p.m. on a Friday or Saturday night or at the A&E department of your local hospital where, following a triumphant battle with a plate glass window, they gather to have their faces sewn back together.

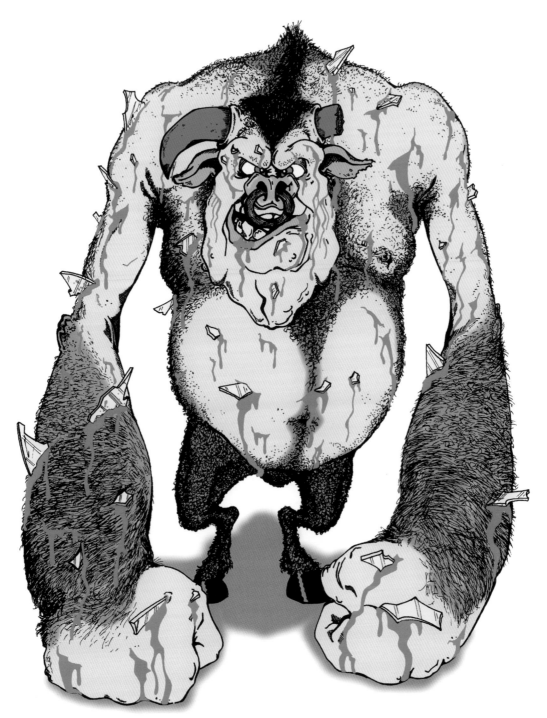

The Bam

The Clart

You may have heard tell of the Clart who visited a doctor for a routine check up and was asked to provide urine, stool and semen samples. The Clart simply removed his underpants and handed them to the doctor with the words, 'I'll be back for them tomorrow.' As you might have guessed, the Clart is a repulsive creature for whom items like soap, shampoo, antiperspirant and toothpaste have the same effect as sulphuric acid. It has to be said that the Clart's mind is just as filthy as its outward appearance and describing what it gets up to in the privacy of its own burrow would almost certainly contravene the Obscene Publications Acts of 1959 and 1964.

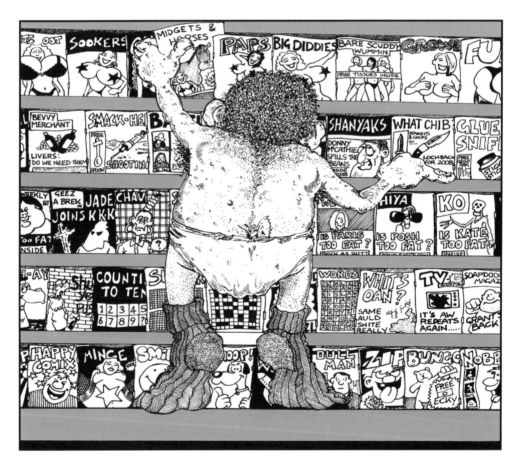

The Clart

The Peely Wally

A pale and sickly creature that spends most of its pathetically short life tucked up in bed watching daytime television, the Peely Wally is the only Baminal to suffer from actual physical symptoms of hypochondria.

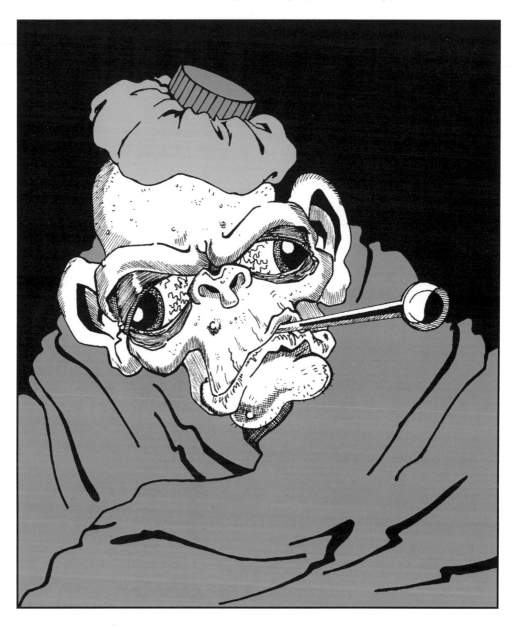

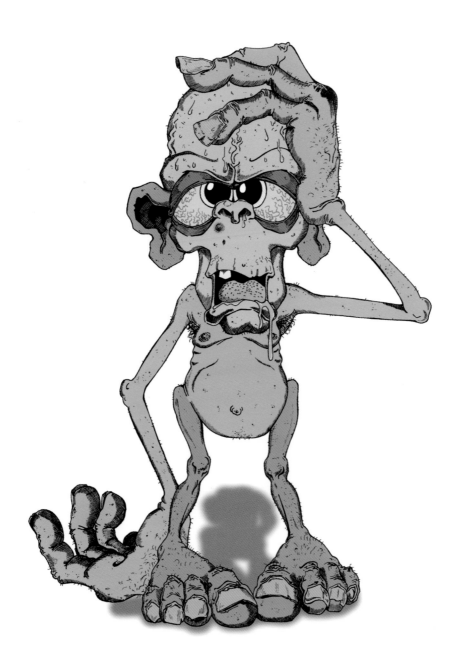

The Peely Wally

The Radge

Driving at 90mph on a busy motorway at night, in the rain, in a car that failed its last MOT for having no brakes. Propping a portable television on top of the taps so that you can watch football in the bath. Walking up to a seven and a half foot tall psychopath and telling him that his girlfriend has a face like a bulldog licking piss off a nettle. These are just a few of the situations that offer the Radge as much concern as you or I would give to a cloudy day. These colourful characters are born without a sense of their own mortality and seem only too willing to steam in where angels fear to tread. It should be pointed out, however, that the Radge rarely conducts itself in such a manner to impress others with acts of courage or heroism. Radges are just phenomenally stupid.

The Radge

The Tartan Army Ant

Whenever the Scottish national football squad is sent to some far-flung corner of the globe to suffer yet another humiliating defeat at the hands of eleven part-time goat herders, they can at the very least count on the undying support of the Tartan Army Ants.

The Tartan

Armed with a sense of optimism that makes Mormons look cynical, they follow their team and cheer with unbridled glee as goal after goal after goal is scored by the opposing side. Having had their hopes of ever attaining anything vaguely resembling a trophy cruelly dashed, they drown their sorrows with enough alcohol to float an aircraft carrier and cheerfully look forward to their next defeat.

Army Ant

The Puffin

First discovered in Scotland in March 2006, Puffins are remarkable creatures who have had to adapt to their environment in a drastically short period of time. Since the ban on smoking in public places was introduced, the Puffins have grown long woolly coats to protect themselves when standing out in the cold and their noses have evolved into rudimentary awnings to keep their cigarettes dry in the rain.

The Puffin

The Chanter

It's in the wee small hours of the morning that you're most likely to hear the sad lament of the Chanter as it staggers on its way back to its burrow after a heavy night of drinking. Despite the fact that the Chanter only knows one song and some of the lyrics to that are slightly suspect, they will happily sing the same verse over and over until someone who has to be up for work in a couple of hours manages to convince them to round up their act with the assistance of a hobnailed boot.

The Chanter

The Farquhar

Thankfully, the Farquhar's numbers never really exceeded any more than a handful at any one time in Scotland. Nevertheless, the few that did exist north of the border throughout the 80s and early 90s caused irreparable damage to the country's industrial base. One of the most remarkable things about the Farquhar is that, despite its inability to fly, it still finds ways to poo on people from a great height. There was an outright cull in May 1997 and Scotland enjoyed a brief period of respite. However, since the opening of the Holyrood Baminal Reserve in Edinburgh, they have managed to creep back in small numbers.

The Farquhar

The Hun and the Tim

Despite their obvious similarities, Huns and Tims do not get along with each other. The real reason for their animosity is a little unclear, although it may have something to do with a battle that took place more than 300 years ago in Ireland, the Queen of England and the Bishop of Rome. Although quite what this has to do with Scottish football remains something of a mystery.

The Hun and the Tim

The Neb

Nebs are naturally curious creatures whose long noses have a pair of finely tuned ears on the end to pick up on conversations that are of little or no concern to them. During the Cold War, they were used by the Ministry of Defence to spy on double agents but these days you're more likely to find them working behind the reception desk at your local medical centre.

The Neb

The Plampher

Despite the fact that Plamphers are rarely seen, their numbers are far from few. If you have ever gone out into the garden to gather in some washing from the line only to find that your underwear has mysteriously disappeared, the chances are that a Plampher has paid a visit during the night. Plamphers are closely related to Chores and have long arms with which to unpeg your shreddies from the line. Quite what they do with the pants when they get them back to their burrows is unclear although it's highly unlikely that you would want them back afterwards.

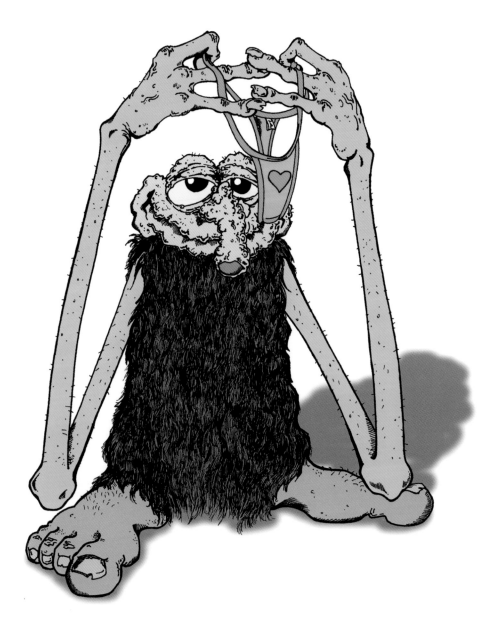

The Plampher

The Choob

If you were to take a close look up a Bam's bum, not only would you be taking your very life in your hands but the chances are that you would find a Choob nestling therein. These parasitic creatures are closely related to the common tapeworm and make a home for themselves in the back passage of more violent and mentally unstable Baminals. There they will massage and tend to the Bam's fragile ego in return for a certain amount of protection and credibility.

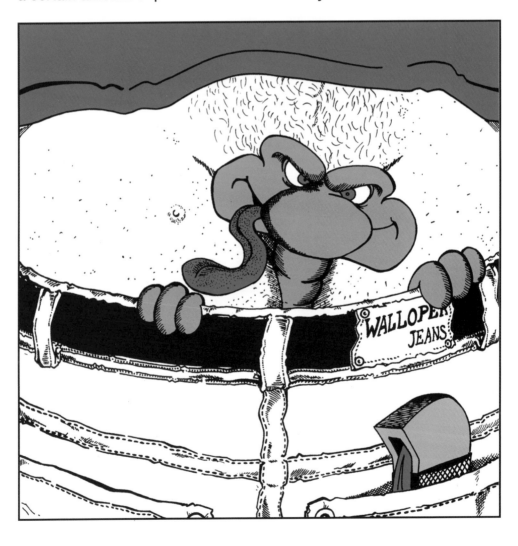

The Choob

The Blether

One of the most commonly encountered Baminals in Scotland is the Blether. Blethers have a unique way of trapping their prey which involves seeking out human beings who appear to be minding their own business and boring them rigid with their views on current affairs. With their victim incapacitated, the Blether begins to feed on their victim's will to live. There is no sure fire way to protect yourself from a Blether attack although it's considered good advice to avoid taxis and going for a haircut.

The Blether

The Ned

Neds can be found throughout the whole of Scotland although the best examples are typically found in and around Glasgow. Neds are easily identifiable by their baseball caps or hooded tops, ridiculous amounts of poor quality jewellery and the vacant expressions on their faces. They spend a great deal of their time consuming alcohol and various narcotic substances in an attempt to turn their brains to porridge which, ironically enough, is their normal state of mind to begin with. Most Neds will carry a knife of some description which they desperately need to compensate for their tiny genitals.

Although Neds are officially recognised as vermin, pressure from Baminal rights activists has meant that they are protected under Scottish law and anyone caught killing a Ned could face a fine of up to fifty pounds.

The Ned

The Jessie

Thunder and lightning, fairground rides, heights, big dogs, spiders, horror films and spicy food – these are just a few of the items on the long, long list of things that scare the shit out of Jessies.

The Jessie

The Dooboo, the Ding'ul and the Dumplin

Dooboos are large slow-witted creatures who, despite their unbelievable stupidity, are generally well liked. Ding'uls can be irritating but are, on the whole, relatively harmless. Dumplins serve no other purpose than to waste the air they breathe and account for 97% of the Scottish Parliament, the remaining 3% being Ding'uls.

It's a sad fact but, were you to take the collective IQ of Scotland's Dooboos, Ding'uls and Dumplins, add them together and multiply by ten, the result would still fail to make double figures. This puts them somewhere between a house brick and a boiled egg.

The Dooboo, the Ding'ul and the Dumplin

The Loch Ness Monster

Last but by no means least is the most famous yet, at the same time, the most rarely seen Baminal in Scotland. The Loch Ness Monster, or Nessie as she is more commonly known, inhabits a twenty-three mile stretch of water in the Highlands. According to Archibald MacDonald, head of the association of Loch Ness hotels, restaurants and gift shops, the best time to catch a glimpse of Nessie is between September and March or, as it's better known, the quiet season. Should you decide to spend a fortnight staring at a big pond and she still fails to put in an appearance, you can always console yourself with a choice of Loch Ness monster souvenirs including, but by no means limited to, soft toys, ceramic statues, tea towels, books, sweets, calendars, T-shirts, stickers, pencil cases, fridge magnets, cruet sets, clocks, golf club covers, slippers, wallpaper, perfume and home pregnancy testing kits.

The Loch Ness Monster

That's yer lot!